WHAT WOULD DEMING DO?

NURTURE GREAT ORGANIZATIONS AND SOCIETIES GUIDED BY W. EDWARDS DEMING'S BEST QUOTES

EDITED BY
NIELS PFLAEGING

BETACODEX PRESS

Other books from BetaCodex Press:
- Organize for Complexity – Niels Pflaeging
- Essays on Beta, Vol. 1 – Niels Pflaeging
- OpenSpace Beta – Silke Hermann/Niels Pflaeging
- What would Drucker do? – Niels Pflaeging (editor)
- Cell Structure Design – Niels Pflaeging/Silke Hermann

2nd, revised and expanded edition 2023
© 2023 Niels Pflaeging, compilation rights only
BetaCodex Press – an imprint of qomenius GmbH
Matthias-Claudius-Strasse 16
D – 65185 Wiesbaden

Editor: Niels Pflaeging
Book design: Niels Pflaeging
Photos: Courtesy of The W. Edwards Deming Institute®
Fonts: League Gothic, IM Fell DW Pica

ISBN Print 978-3-9484-7120-0
ISBN E-Book 978-3-9484-7121-7

For attractive volume discounts on BetaCodex Press books,
which start at 10 copies, get in touch with
contact@betacodexpress.com

Visit our website: betacodexpress.com
Check out our web shop at redforty2.com/shop

CONTENTS

ABOUT DEMING

W. Edwards Deming (1900-1993) was perhaps the first to apply rigorous systems thinking and systems theory to entire organizations. He did so starting in 1950 in Japan, where his work soon gained wide-spread attention. Many Japanese firms, including Toyota, were impacted by Deming's thinking. This culminated in what would later be called the Japanese economic miracle.

Deming condemned management by objectives, incentive systems, merit ranking, appraisal, and command-and-control. A charismatic, witty and humorous figure, he became well-known in the West only much later, when, in 1980, he was featured in an NBC TV documentary called *If Japan can... Why can't we?*

Already in his 80s, Deming became hugely influential to the international Total Quality movement of the 1980s and 1990s. But the decidedly systemic nature of his thinking became sidelined there, after a while.

Deming consolidated his thinking in the books *Out of the Crisis* (1986) and *The New Economics* (1993). He continued teaching and consulting throughout the world until his death at the age of 93, in December 1993.

Deming remains one of the greatest and one of the most wide-ranging thinkers in the history of organizational leadership.

Deming in his kitchen, 1980s

"Prevailing practices of management and education have crushed the individual. Toddlers at the age of three are crushed by prizes for costumes, grades in school, gold stars for athletics. Forces of destruction continue onward through further schooling, and onward into the work place through life, robbing the individual of joy in learning and joy in work."

From a memo to a consulting client, December 1989

PEOPLE AT WORK

Deming in the 1950s

"People are entitled
to joy in work."

"Numerical goals set
for other people, without
a road map to reach the goal,
have effects opposite
to the effects sought."

"People with targets
and jobs dependent upon
meeting them will likely meet
the targets – even if
they have to destroy
the enterprise to do it."

"Absenteeism is largely
a function of supervision.
If people feel important
to a job, they will
come to work."

"The basic fault of the annual appraisal is that it penalizes people for normal variation of a system."

"The merit rating nourishes short-term performance, annihilates long-term planning, builds fear, demolishes teamwork, [and] nourishes rivalry and politics. It leaves people bitter, crushed, bruised, battered, desolate, despondent, dejected, feeling inferior, some even depressed, unfit for work for weeks after receipt of rating, unable to comprehend why they are inferior. It is unfair, as it ascribes to the people in a group differences that may be caused totally by the system that they work in."

"What are the big losses? Answer: the so-called merit systems — actually, destroyer of people. M.B.O., management by the numbers, quotas, failure to optimize the various activities and divisions of a company as a system, business plans in terms of a matrix of targets, without regard to the whole plan as a system of improvement."

"The most valuable 'currency' of any organization is the initiative and creativity of its members. Every leader has the solemn moral responsibility to develop these to the maximum in all his people. This is the leader's highest priority."

"The greatest waste [...]
is failure to use the abilities of people.
One need only listen to a tape
of a meeting with production
workers to learn about their
frustrations and about the
contribution that they are eager
to make. Anyone would be impressed
to observe how articulate most
production workers are, in spite of
criticisms of our schools."

"Give the work force a chance
to work with pride, and
the 3 per cent that apparently
don't care will erode itself
by peer pressure."

"Why waste knowledge? [...]
No company can afford to waste knowledge. Failure of management to break down barriers between activities [...] is one way to waste knowledge. People that are not working together are not contributing their best to the company. People as they work together, feeling secure in the job reinforce their knowledge and efforts. Their combined output, when they are working together, is more than the sum of their separate."

"A manager of people needs to understand that all people are different. This is not ranking people. He needs to understand that the performance of anyone is governed largely by the system that he works in, the responsibility of management."

"Our prevailing system of management has destroyed our people. People are born with intrinsic motivation, self-respect, dignity, curiosity to learn, joy in learning. The forces of destruction begin with toddlers – a prize for the best Halloween costume, grades in school, gold stars – and on up through the university. On the job people, teams, and divisions are ranked, reward for the top, punishment for the bottom. Management by Objectives, quotas, incentive pay, business plans, put together separately, division by division, cause further loss, unknown and unknowable."

"People generally want to do the right thing, but in a large organization, they frequently don't really understand what is the right thing."

"Mobility of labor [...] is another serious problem. A strong contributing factor is dissatisfaction with the job, inability to take pride in the work. People stay at home or look around for another job when they can not take pride in their work. Absenteeism and mobility are largely creations of poor management."

"The aim of leadership should be
to improve the performance of man
and machine, to improve quality,
to increase output, and simultaneous-
ly to bring pride of workmanship
to people. Put in a negative way,
the aim of leadership is not merely to
find and record failures of men, but
to remove the causes of failure:
to help people to do a better job
with less effort."

"What is at the heart
of the transformation?
It is the release of the power
of intrinsic motivation.
How? By creating joy,
pride, happiness in work;
joy and pride in learning."

"One is born with a
natural inclination to learn
and to be innovative.
One inherits a right
to enjoy his work.
Psychology helps us
to nurture and preserve
these positive innate
attributes of people."

"Fear takes a horrible toll. Fear is all around, robbing people of their pride, hurting them, robbing them of a chance to contribute to the company. It is unbelievable what happens when you unloose fear."

"Another unknowable figure is the multiplying effect that comes from an employee group that is able to make a contribution to the company as a team. They see their job as important. They are helping the company to improve. They take pride in their work. Their lives change – I have seen it happen."

"Pay is not a motivator."

"A company could put a top man at every position and be swallowed by a competitor with people only half as good, but who are working together."

In a note written in April 1992, Deming looked back to his time in Japan soon after WWII: "Japan was in a crisis. The crisis was visible, the country blown to bits, destroyed by fire. Our country [the United States] is in a worse crisis because it is invisible. Japanese top management asked me in 1950 to come to help. Japan soon became an economic power. The secret:

> Management of a system, cooperation
> between components, not competition.
> Management of people.

We suffer from evil styles of management, such as ranking people, divisions, plants (creating competition between people), management by results, failure to understand cooperation in a system in which everybody wins. Transformation is required, not mere change. Transformation requires Profound Knowledge."

LEARNING

Deming with businessmen, geishas and Kenichi Koyanagi
(managing director of the Union of Japanese Scientists
and Engineers JUSE), in 1951

"We are being ruined
by the best efforts
of people who are doing
the wrong thing."

"A goal can never help
anybody to do a better job."

"Knowledge is theory.
We should be thankful if action of
management is based on theory.
Knowledge has temporal spread.
Information is not knowledge.
The world is drowning
in information, but is slow
in acquisition of knowledge.
There is no substitute
for knowledge."

"Theory is a window to another world. Theory leads to prediction. Without prediction, experience and examples teach nothing. Experience teaches nothing without theory. It's only by theory that experience teaches anything."

"In this country, in the Western World, economists have taught us that competition is a way of life – competition solves problems. In Japan – I can speak to it after all – it's cooperation. We may learn, sometime, whether to use cooperation, not competition. Actually, we do not believe in competition. We say that we do, but we don't."

"I see [people] thinking
that one should take up
a vocation and don't study
theory. They don't see
anything but nonsense in
theory. So many people
do not understand what
education is."

"Learning is not
compulsory...
neither is survival."

"Learning is not compulsory;
it's voluntary.
Improvement is not
compulsory; it's voluntary.
But to survive,
we must learn."

"Many of us deceive ourselves into the supposition that we need constant updating to cope with the rapidly changing future. Not so.
You cannot, by watching every moment of television or by reading every newspaper acquire a glimpse of what the future holds. To put it another way, information, no matter how complete and speedy, is not knowledge. Cramming your heads full of information for an examination. That's not knowledge, that's not learning. It has no temporal spread. Knowledge must involve the future, and have explanation of the past. Knowledge comes from theory. Without theory there's no way to use the information that comes to us on the instant."

"What's a school of business for? What a school of business does is to teach the students how business is conducted today, how to get a job in the system, in the style of management that persists today. What the school of business ought to teach is transformation, but who there could teach it? Who would know?"

"It is not enough
to do your best;
you must know what to do,
and then do your best."

"I hope not.
That would be the worst
thing you could do."

Answering the question if he ever
studied American business methods.

"We are here to have fun, to learn, to work together – and to make a difference."

"Our schools must preserve and nurture the yearning for learning that everyone is born with. Grades and gold stars destroy this yearning for learning.

Joy in learning comes not so much from what is learned, but from learning. It's fun to learn, if you learn knowledge. Not fun to learn information."

"Only one person
can do your own study
and that's you."

"Does experience help?
No! Not if we are doing
the wrong things."

"Anyone can improve his work, they say, if he has enough information. The fact is that a figure by itself provides no information, has no meaning, no interpretation, in the absence of theory. In short, there is no substitute for knowledge, and a figure by itself is not knowledge."

"Everyone doing his best
is not the answer.
Everybody is doing his best.
It is necessary that people
understand the reason for the
changes that are necessary.
Moreover, there must be
consistency of understanding
and of effort."

"Another unfortunate drag
on American management is
American schools of business
that lead students to suppose that
a manager need not know anything.
There is in most American schools
of business a loss of respect
for the fundamentals of knowledge
such as economics, history, theory
of law, psychology, mathematics,
statistical methods."

"I'm afraid that what [American business schools] teach is continuance of our present methods of management, which are failures. They teach how to fail, how to continue to fail."

"I love my work –
continue learning,
advancement in presentation,
advancement
in understanding."

Answering the question how
he kept going at age 93

"The first step is transformation of the individual. This transformation is discontinuous. It comes from understanding of the system of profound knowledge.

The individual, transformed, will perceive new meaning to his life, to events, to numbers, to interactions between people. Once the individual understands the system of profound knowledge, he will apply its principles in every kind of relationship with other people. He will have a basis for judgment of his own decisions and for transformation of the organizations that he belongs to."

In a memo from 1978, to the dean of a business school, Deming wrote: "Everyone knows that the economy of the United States has not maintained leadership in productivity that the world requires for balance of commerce. There are doubtless many reasons for this poor performance, but one of them surely lies in the failure of American management to keep abreast of modern methods of management. Innovation in America has not kept up with the Japanese. Relations between the American production-worker and American management presents a sad spectacle. By contrast, in Japan, the contribution of the production worker and the contribution of management are a joint effort. All people work together toward the same end, even though the motivation may in some part be selfish. The greater the productivity, the better the economic lot of everybody. This is a simple principle and it is learned in Japan at an early age."

SUSTAINABILITY

Deming lecturing in Japan, 1955

"Why are we here?
We are here to make
another world."

"The aim proposed here
for any organization is
for everybody to gain –
stockholders, employees,
suppliers, customers, community, the environment –
over the long term."

"It is important that an aim never be defined in terms of a specific activity or method. It must always relate to a better life for everyone."

"Competitors, instead of trying to get share of market from each other, should try to expand the market. And both win."

"It is no longer socially acceptable to dump employees on to the heap of unemployed. Loss of market, and resulting unemployment are not foreordained. They are not inevitable. They are man-made."

"Japanese industry has proved to the world that statistical techniques have their best application where raw materials and machines are scarce. It is well to remember that a 10% increase in production, with no increase in raw materials or machines or floor space, is equivalent to the discovery of vast new national resources, such as new veins of copper, new veins of coal."

"A wise customer will listen to the supplier. Listen to the suggestions of the supplier. In other words, they work together as a system."

"Paper profits do not
make the pie bigger.
They give you a bigger piece.
You take it from somebody
else. It doesn't help
the society."

Deming proposed not just to treat organizations as systems. But to also take relations between organizations, within countries and between countries into view.

He wrote: "What is a system? A system is a network of interdependent components that work together to try to accomplish the aim of the system. A system must have an aim. Without an aim, there is no system. The aim of the system must be clear to everyone in the system. The aim must include plans for the future. The aim is a value judgment. (We are of course talking here about a man-made system.)"

And: "If economists understood the theory of a system, and the role of cooperation to optimization, they would no longer teach and preach salvation through adversarial competition. They would, instead, lead us into optimization, in which everybody would come out ahead, including competitors."

SYSTEMS

Deming working over tea with executives of the Union
of Japanese Scientists and Engineers (JUSE), 1956

"Efforts of the various divisions in a company, each given a job, are not additive. Their efforts are interdependent. One division to achieve its goal may, left to itself, kill off another division."

"A system must be managed.
It will not manage itself.
Left to themselves in the Western
world, components become selfish,
competitive, independent profit cen-
ters, and thus destroy the system. [...]
The secret is cooperation between
components toward the aim of the
organization. We can not afford
the destructive effect
of competition."

"You must not run your organization as a functional hierarchy. You must understand it as a system."

n.a.

"If the problem is caused by
the way the process is designed
(a management responsibility),
the tweaking done by the employee
may alter the system in such a way
that future products or services are
even worse. The correction addresses
the wrong problem and winds up
doing more harm than good.
It's counter-intuitive to believe that
your best workers, doing their best,
could make things worse. Best efforts
won't cut it; better management of
the system is needed."

"Eighty-five percent
of the reasons for failure are
deficiencies in the systems
and process rather than
the employee. The role of
management is to change the
process rather than badgering
individuals to do better."

Deming used the 85/15 ratio to attribute fault,
after learning it from Dr. Juran. It wasn't until the late 1980s
or early 1990s that he revised it to 94%/6% and later 97%/3%,
reflecting his thinking on systems and variation.

"A bad system
will beat a good person
every time."

"We know how to optimize pieces, but optimization of a larger system is difficult."

"It is a mistake to assume
that if everybody does his job,
it will be all right.
The whole system
may be in trouble."

"To successfully respond
to the myriad of changes
that shake the world, transformation into a new style
of management is required.
The route to take is what
I call profound knowledge –
knowledge for leadership
of transformation."

"The prevailing style
of management must
undergo transformation.
A system cannot understand
itself. The transformation
requires a view from outside."

With "view from the outside" Deming refers
to the System of Profound Knowledge and his 14 Points –
see the final chapter of this book.

"Transformation
is not automatic.
It must be learned;
it must be led."

"The worker
is not the problem.
The problem is at the top!
Management!"

"People don't like to make mistakes.
Change the system and the workers are suddenly a lot happier. They're no longer being blamed for what they have no control over."

"People work in the system. Management creates the system."

"Sure we want best efforts,
but best efforts must be guided
by theory and knowledge. Those who
only give us best efforts – let them
stay at home, in bed, and sleep late.
We would all be better off.
They only tamper and make things
worse. When these approaches
[quick fixes] are used without the
benefit of profound knowledge,
they are counter-productive."

"It is not necessary to change. Survival is not mandatory."

"The supposition is prevalent
the world over that there would be
no problems in production or service
if only our production workers
would do their jobs in the way that
they were taught. Pleasant dreams.
The workers are handicapped
by the system, and the system
belongs to the management."

"94% of the problems
in business are system-driven
and only 6%
are people-driven."

"Evaluation of performance, merit rating, or annual review. These traditional appraisal systems reward people who do well in the system. They do not reward attempts to improve the system."

"The system that people
work in and the interaction
with people may account
for 90 or 95 percent
of performance."

"A flow diagram is actually an organization chart. It shows how the different components, each with its expert knowledge, work together for the gain of all. If the components become competitive, the system is destroyed. Everybody loses. [...] The greater the interdependence between components, the greater the need for communication and cooperation between them."

"Management of a system requires knowledge of the interrelationships between all the components within the system. And of the people that work in it."

"Most people think of management as a chain of command. My theory says that the system is like an orchestra, not an army. Every one in an orchestra supports the other players. Each player watches not only the conductor, but also each other and the whole system.

The system needs a conductor, not a general. It needs someone who harmonizes the talents and abilities of each part of the system. Each player in the orchestra knows that he is part of a system, even when he plays solo. He is not there to attract attention to himself. He succeeds when he supports the other players."

"Any group should have as its aim optimization over time of the larger system that the group operates in. Anything less than optimization of the whole system will bring eventual loss to every component in the system."

"What is a leader? As I use the term here, the job of a leader is to accomplish transformation of his organization. He possesses knowledge; he himself has been transformed. He has personality and persuasive power. How may he accomplish transformation? First, he has theory. He understands why the transformation would bring gain to the organization and to all the people that his organization deals with, the customers, suppliers, environment. Second, he feels compelled to accomplish the transformation as an obligation to himself and to his organization. Third, he is a practical man. He has a plan, step by step, and can explain it in simple terms."

"A system can not
understand itself. One may
learn a lot about ice,
yet know very
little about water."

At a presentation at Fordham University, in 1992: "We're living in a prison. Under the tyranny of the prevailing style of management. A style of interaction between people, between teams, between divisions, between competitors. We need to throw overboard our theories and practices of the present, and build afresh. We must throw overboard the idea that competition is a necessary way of life. In place of competition, we need cooperation. We need to examine the effects of ideas that govern us today and to learn better ways." And: "Transformation is required in government, industry and education. Management is in a stable state. Transformation is required to move out of the present state. Not mere patchwork of the present system. Throw overboard what we have. Of course we have to stamp out fires where they occur, but stamping out fires is not improvement. That's just putting [things] back to where you were in the first place."

SOCIETIES

Deming enjoying a martini during
a holiday in the 1960s

"American management thinks that they can just copy from Japan—but they don't know what to copy!"

"Dependence on protection
by tariffs and laws to
'buy American' only
encourages incompetence."

"A common disease that afflicts management and government administration the world over is the impression that 'Our problems are different.' They are different, to be sure, but the principles that will help to improve quality of product and of service are universal in nature."

"Export anything
to a friendly country
except American
management."

"No community need be poor
if it has people
and good management.
No country need be poor
if it has people
and good management."

"Unfortunately, wrong styles of management move freely across the international borders."

"Government service
is to be judged on equity
as well as on efficiency."

"The responsibility of government is equity. If we do not keep equity in the forefront, we will destroy our society."

"The source of innovation is freedom. All we have –new knowledge, invention – comes from freedom. Somebody responsible only to himself has the heaviest responsibility. 'You cannot plan to make a discovery,' Irving Langmuir said. Discoveries and new knowledge come from freedom. When somebody is responsible only to himself, [has] only himself to satisfy, then you'll have invention, new thought, now product, new design, new ideas."

Irving Langmuir (1881-1957) was an American chemist, physicist, and engineer. He was awarded the Nobel Prize in Chemistry in 1932 for his work in surface chemistry

"Paper profits do not
make bread: improvement of
quality and productivity do.
They make a contribution
to better material living
for all people, here
and everywhere."

In 1986, Deming wrote: "There is much talk about the need to improve quality and productivity. Moreover, everyone knows exactly how to go about it. It is for other people to accomplish, not for me. In the eyes of many people in management, the big trouble is that a lot of employees in operations and in management as well are careless and neglectful on the job. One writer has the solution – hold all employees accountable for job behavior as well as for the results expected of them. The fact is that performance appraisal, management by the numbers, M.B.O., and work standards have already devastated Western industry. More of the same could hardly be a solution. The annual rating of performance has devastated Western industry. Work standards double the cost of the operations that they are applied to."

EXCELLENCE

"My mother was
my biggest role model.
She taught me to hate waste.
We never wasted anything."

"When I was to travel in Japan,

    17:25: leave Taku City
    19:23: arrive Hakata,
           change trains
    19:24: leave Hakata
    21:20: arrive Osaka

One minute to change trains.
No problem, no alternative plan.
Why would you need an alternate
plan? Think of being able to plan,
with one plan, not two or three."

"Quality is
pride of workmanship."

"Management has failed in this country. It is continuing to fail. It insists on ranking people with management-mandated performance criteria, the refuge of the destitute. It leads to reward at the top and punishment at the bottom. It is a ruinous, chaotic system that removes joy from the workplace and leaves in its place, mistrust and stress."

"What you've got is this chain reaction. As you improve the quality, costs go down. You can lower your price. You capture the market with quality and price. Americans do not understand it. Americans think that as you improve quality, you increase your costs."

"Improvement of quality transfers waste of man-hours and of machine-time into the manufacture of good product and better service. The result is a chain reaction– lower costs, better competitive position, happier people on the job, jobs, and more jobs."

"The customer is the most important part of the production line. Without him, there is no production line."

"Quality control departments
have taken the job of quality
away from the people
that can contribute most
to quality – management,
supervisors, managers
of purchasing, and
production workers."

"Best efforts are essential. Unfortunately, best efforts, people charging this way and that way without guidance of principles, can do a lot of damage."

"Money and time spent for training will be ineffective unless inhibitors to good work are removed."

"Support of top management is not sufficient. It is not enough that top management commit themselves for life to quality and productivity. They must know what it is that they are committed to – that is, what they must do. These obligations can not be delegated. Support is not enough: action is required."

"The transformation
can only be accomplished
by man, not by hardware
(computers, gadgets,
automation, new machinery).
A company can not
buy its way into quality."

"The idea of a merit rating is alluring. The sound of the words captivates the imagination: pay for what you get; get what you pay for; motivate people to do their best, for their own good.

The effect is exactly the opposite of what the words promise. Everyone propels himself forward, or tries to, for his own good, on his own life preserver. The organization is the loser.

The merit rating rewards people that conform to the system. It does not reward attempts to improve the system. Don't rock the boat."

"Standardization does not mean
that we all wear the same color
and weave of cloth, eat standard
sandwiches, or live in standard rooms
with standard furnishings.
Homes of infinite variety of design
are built with a few types of bricks,
and with lumber of standard sizes,
and with water and heating pipes and
fittings of standard dimensions."

"Innovation comes
from the producer –
not from the customer."

"Customer expectations?
Nonsense. No customer ever
asked for the electric light,
the pneumatic tire, the VCR,
or the CD. All customer
expectations are only what
you and your competitor
have led him to expect.
He knows nothing else."

"Top management should
publish a resolution
that no one will lose his job
for contribution to quality
and productivity."

"Quality comes not from inspection, but from improvement of the production process."

"Inspection does not improve the quality, nor guarantee quality. Inspection is too late. The quality, good or bad, is already in the product. As Harold F. Dodge said, 'You can not inspect quality into a product.' The quality is there or it isn't by the time it's inspected."

Harold French Dodge (1893--1976) was an
American statistician and one of the principal architects
of the science of statistical quality control

"Our system of
make-and-inspect,
which if applied to making
toast would be expressed:
'You burn, I'll scrape.'"

"No one knows the cost
of a defective product –
don't tell me you do.
You know the cost of
replacing it, but not the cost
of a dissatisfied customer."

"Defects are not free.
Somebody makes them,
and gets paid
for making them."

"Quality is made in
the board room.
A worker can deliver
lower quality, but she cannot
deliver quality better
than the system allows."

"Profit in business comes from repeat customers, customers that boast about your project or service, and that bring friends with them."

"It will not suffice
to have customers that are
merely satisfied. An unhappy
customer will switch.
Unfortunately, a satisfied
customer may also switch,
on the theory that he could
not lose much,
and might gain."

"The moral is that it is
necessary to innovate,
to predict needs of the
customer, give him more.
He that innovates and is
lucky will take the market."

"The production worker
is already interested.
Has never been interested
in anything but quality and
productivity. That is his life.
He knows that poor quality
in the hands of a customer
may cost him his job. The
management doesn't care.
Nobody ever lost a job
in management for doing
nothing about quality."

"Declining productivity
and quality means your unit
production costs stay high but
you don't have as much
to sell. Your workers don't
want to be paid less, so to
maintain profits, you increase
your prices. That's inflation."

"The workers have always been involved. The only ones that have been involved. That's the problem."

"To copy an example of success, without understanding the success with the aid of theory may lead to disaster."

"Computerized quality
information systems provide
the vital link between
high technology and effective
decision-making.

I wish that management
were as simple as that."

"There are four prongs of quality and four ways to improve quality of product and service:

- Innovation in product and service;
- Innovation in process;
- Improvement of existing product and service;
- Improvement of existing process.

The common mistake is the supposition that quality is ensured by No. 4, improvement of process, that operations going off without blemish on the factory floor, in the bank, in the hotel will ensure quality. Good operations are essential, yet they do not ensure quality. Quality is made in the boardroom."

"A good question for anybody in business to ask is What business are we in? To do well what we are doing – i.e., to turn out a good product, or good service, whatever it be? Yes, of course, but this is not enough. We must keep asking – What product or service would help our customers more? We must think about the future. What will we be making 5 years from now? 10 years from now?"

"Much automation and much new machinery is a source of poor quality and high cost, helping to put us out of business. Much of it, if it performs as intended, is built for twice the capacity that is needed."

"Putting out fires
is not improvement.
Finding a point out of
control, finding the special
cause and removing it, is only
putting the process back to
where it was in the first place.
It is not improvement
of the process."

"There are conferences almost any day in this country on the subject of productivity, mostly concerned with gadgets and measures of productivity. As William E. Conway said, measurements of productivity are like accident statistics. They tell you that there is a problem, but they don't do anything about accidents."

William E. Conway (1926-2011) started working at Nashua Corp. in 1954, and rose to become the company's president and chairman. Conway was strongly influenced by Deming, and became consultant and writer on quality in his later career.

"I may remind you that, according to Japanese testimony, it was the statistical control of quality that brought about the revolution of quality and efficiency of production in Japan, which began in 1950. These methods affect all aspects of production, from raw material to finished product, plus consumer research and re-design of product, and design of new products. One feature, especially applicable to production, is techniques by which to distinguish between (a) special causes of variation of quality and economic loss, which the worker himself can correct on statistical signal, and (b) faults of the system, which only management can correct. Statistical methods thus assist management and production-worker in Japan to pull together."

W. Edwards Deming, August 1978

MEASURING

"It is wrong to suppose
that if you can't measure it,
you can't manage it –
a costly myth."

"Management by numerical
goal is an attempt
to manage without knowledge
of what to do, and in fact
is usually management
by fear."

"A numerical goal leads
to distortion and faking,
especially when the system
is not capable of meeting the
goal. Anybody will meet the
quota (goal) allotted to him.
He is not responsible for
the losses so generated."

"Numerical goals.
No method.
No method suggested.
Just numerical goals drawn
out of the sky. Such nonsense
in high places. Think of
the harm done by those
numerical goals put out."

"Performance of the individual cannot be measured, except on a long-term basis, for which I mean 15, 18, 20 years."

"Where there is fear you do not get honest figures."

"Management by results —
like driving a car by looking
in rear view mirror."

"Management by results is not the way to get good results, it is the way to get worse results. Work on causes, not on results. This kind of management is tampering."

"Reward for good performance may be the same as reward to the weatherman for a nice day. [...] You cannot measure performance. Appraisal of people is ruinous."

"Data are not taken for museum purposes; they are taken as a basis for doing something. If nothing is to be done with the data, then there is no use in collecting any. The ultimate purpose of taking data is to provide a basis for action or a recommendation for action. The step intermediate between the collection of data and the action is prediction."

"Performance [of people]
cannot be measured. You only
measure the combined effect
of the system and his efforts.
You cannot untangle the two.
It is very important, I believe,
that performance cannot
be measured."

"The most important figures that one needs for management are unknown or unknowable."

"He that would run
his company on visible figures
alone will in time
have neither company
nor figures."

"Recognition of the distinction between a stable system and an unstable one is vital for management. A stable system is one whose performance is predictable. It appears to be in statistical control."

In his foreword to the book *Deming Management at Work*, Deming wrote: "The change required is transformation, change of state, metamorphosis, in industry, education, and government. The transformation will restore the individual by the abolishment of grades in school on up through the university; by abolishment of the annual appraisal of people on the job, MBO [Management by Objectives], quotas for production, incentive pay, competition between people, competition between divisions, and other forms of sub-optimization. The transformation is not stamping out fires, solving problems, nor cosmetic improvements. The transformation must be led by top management."

MANAGERS

"Management must
constantly improve
the system. This obligation
never ceases."

"The prevailing – and foolish – attitude is that a good manager can be a good manager anywhere, with no special knowledge of the production process he's managing. A man with a financial background may know nothing about manufacturing shoes or cars, but he's put in charge anyway."

"A good manager
of people capitalizes on the
family background, abilities,
capabilities, and hopes of
his people. He tries to give
everybody a chance to
take pride in his work,
joy in his work."

"It is easy to manage
a business in an expanding
market, and easy to suppose
that economic conditions can
only grow better and better.
In contrast with expectations,
we find, on looking back, that
we have been on an economic
decline for three decades.
It is easy to date an earth-
quake, but not a decline."

"It is management's job to direct the efforts of all components toward the aim of the system. The first step is clarification: everyone in the organization must understand the aim of the system, and how to direct his efforts toward it. Everyone must understand the damage and loss to the whole organization from a team that seeks to become a selfish, independent, profit center."

"Long-term commitment to new learning and new philosophy is required of any management that seeks transformation. The timid and the faint-hearted, and people that expect quick results, are doomed to disappointment."

"Part of America's industrial problems is the aim of its corporate managers. Most American executives think they are in the business to make money, rather than products or service... The Japanese corporate credo, on the other hand, is that a company should become the world's most efficient provider of whatever product and service it offers. Once it becomes the world leader and continues to offer good products, profits follow."

"If you don't understand how
to run an efficient operation,
new machinery will just
give you new problems of
operation and maintenance.
The sure way to increase
productivity is to better
administrate man
and machine."

"Is your company suffering from overjustification? Of course you don't have the figures. There are not any figures for the most important losses. Somebody asked a question this morning: 'If one performs very well, how would you reward him?' Why should you reward him? It would be demoralization to reward him. [...] What are the losses in your company from overjustification? Paying for suggestions, maybe? Rewarding extraordinary performance? Is that costing you? Of course you don't know. Nobody knows."

"Management by walking around is hardly ever effective. The reason is that someone in management, walking around, has little idea about what questions to ask, and usually does not pause long enough at any spot to get the right answer."

"Short-term profits are
not reliable indicator of
performance of management.
Anybody can pay dividends
by deferring maintenance,
cutting out research,
or acquiring another
company."

"Mobility from one company to another creates prima donnas for quick results. Mobility annihilates teamwork, so vital for continued existence."

"Management must understand design of product and of service, procurement of materials, problems of production, process control, and barriers on the job that rob people of their birthright: the right to pride of workmanship."

**"I leave you
with five little words:
We only did our best."**

Words of closure at the end
of one of Deming's 4-day seminars

Deming advocated a System of Profound Knowledge, which would benefit anyone, any organization, and divisions within organizations. This system consisted of four interrelated parts:

1. Appreciation of a system
2. Theory of variation
3. Theory of knowledge
4. Knowledge of psychology

Deming explained: "One need not be eminent in any part nor in all four parts in order to understand it and apply it. The 14 points for management in industry, education, and government [shown on the following pages] follow naturally as application of this outside knowledge, for transformation from the present style of Western management to one of optimization." And: "The various segments of the System of Profound Knowledge proposed here cannot be separated. They interact with each other. Thus, knowledge of psychology is incomplete without knowledge of variation."

DEMING'S
14 POINTS

01 Create constancy of purpose toward improvement of product and service, with the aim to become competitive and to stay in business, and to provide jobs.

02 Adopt the new philosophy. We are in a new economic age. Western management must awaken to the challenge, must learn their responsibilities, and take on leadership for change.

03 Cease dependence on inspection to achieve quality. Eliminate the need for inspection on a mass basis by building quality into the product in the first place.

04 End the practice of awarding business on the basis of price tag. Instead, minimize total cost. Move toward a single supplier for any one item, on a long-term relationship of loyalty and trust.

05 Improve constantly and forever the system of production and service, to improve quality and productivity, and thus constantly decrease cost.

06 Institute training on the job.

07 Institute leadership. The aim of supervision should be to help people and machines and gadgets to do a better job. Supervision of management is in need of overhaul, as well as supervision of prod. workers.

08 Drive out fear, so that everyone may work effectively for the company.

09 Break down barriers between departments. People in research, design, sales, and production must work as a team, to foresee problems of production and in use that may be encountered with the product or service.

10 Eliminate slogans, exhortations, and targets for the work force asking for zero defects or new levels of productivity. Such exhortations only create adversarial relationships, as the bulk of the causes of low quality and low productivity belong to the system and thus lie beyond the power of the work force.

11 a) Eliminate work standards (quotas) on the factory floor. Substitute leadership. b) Eliminate management by objective. Eliminate management by numbers, numerical goals. Substitute leadership.

12 a) Remove barriers that rob the hourly worker of his right to pride of workmanship. The responsibility of supervision must be changed from sheer numbers to quality. b) Remove barriers that rob people in management and in engineering of their right to pride of workmanship. This means, *inter alia,* abolishment of the annual or merit rating and of mngmt. by objective.

13 Institute a vigorous program of education and self-improvement.

14 Put everybody in the company to work to accomplish the transformation. The transformation is everybody's job.

MY DEMING

It was around 1978 that W. Edwards Deming turned to writing and publishing about the topic of transformation of management. Nuggets on management theory had appeared in his books and in his many articles from the previous forty years, even though his writings were mostly about statistics and sampling theory. But it was the speaking, teaching and publishing from the last 16 years of his life that brought Deming's practical and philosophical contributions to the world to full fruition, internationally. With some notable exceptions, the quotes in this book come from this last period of Deming's life. As you can see from the pages of this book, Deming made excellent use of those years.

I strongly believe, however, that Deming's work and message are now more contemporary than ever. And that is for one very simple reason: Because the transformation of thinking, organizations and systems that Deming so vigorously demanded has not yet occurred. While our problems have been aggravated, by and large, we have not overcome command-and-control, systemic sub-optimization, and drastic waste of human potential, in both work and our societies.

Three decades after Deming's death, we are still hesitant of putting Deming's *System of Profound Knowledge* to work. At the same time, unsustainable patterns and practices in business and societies are looming large, and climate change has gathered speed, threatening human existence and our democracies. I believe that Deming's work entails the complete solution to all the above mentioned problems. I believe that Deming very clearly outlined what is needed, and what kind of systems design based on what principles we must strive for. Deming matters, now more than ever. We should listen to what Deming said and did. And put his teaching's to good effect, at last.

It is staggering to me, however, that, in spite of the remarkable clarity of his words, and the coherence of his teachings, Deming's work did not directly lead to full-fledged transformation anywhere, beyond Japan. On the bright side, Deming's thinking has been incorporated into new methods that allow full-fledged transformation of entire systems with thousands or tens of thousands of people. I am firmly convinced that the world now possesses practical approaches to make such transformations happen everywhere: concepts like *OpenSpace Beta*, *Cell Structure Design* and *Relative Targets* are consistent with Deming's teachings, and available to everyone. These new concepts offer resolve. We now also have the means to accelerate education, using virtual approaches to learning like *qomenius*.

We need to employ Deming's thinking, and combine it with methods that are consistent with his thinking. Deming's wisdom cannot be lost. We need him now. More than ever.

Deming teaching in Japan, 1951

SOURCES

The source of each quote is indicated at the bottom of the quote's page – see title abbreviations below.

Quoted books by & about W. Edwards Deming:

Deming, W. Edwards: Out of the Crisis (OotC)

Deming, W. Edwards: The New Economics for Industry, Government, Education (TNE)

Deming, W. Edwards: Quality, Productivity, and Competitive Position (QPCP)

Orsini, Joyce: The Essential Deming (TED)

Kilian, Cecilia: The World of W. Edwards Deming (WoD)

Latzko. William J./Saunders, David M.: Four Days with Dr. Deming (4DwD)

Voehl, Frank: Deming The Way We Knew Him (DW)

Walton, Mary: The Deming Management Method (DMM)

Delavigne, Kenneth T./Robertson, J. Daniel: Deming's Profound Changes (DPC)

Aguayo, Rafael: Dr. Deming – the American Who Taught the Japanese About Quality (DD)

Quotations of Dr. Deming: The Little Blue Book (LBB)

Other quoted sources:

Article: Industry Week Interview, Management Today Does Not Know What Its Job Is (IWI) *continued*

SOURCES

... continued

Article: Drastic Changes for Western Management, by W. Edwards Deming, 1986 (DC)

Article: Ronald D. Snee, W. Edwards Deming's 'Making Another World' (Snee)

Article: People Weekly Magazine, May 8, 1980 (PWM)

Article: If Americans Don't Want To Listen to Me, It's Their Funeral, Washington Post (WP)

Article: New York Times, He taught the Japanese (NYT)

Article: Chicago Tribune, Deming, guru of quality management, dies at 93 (CT)

Article: Introduction to The Fifth Discipline (Revised Edition) by Peter Senge, quoted from a personal note by Deming to Senge (Senge)

Article: Transcript of a recorded conversation between Russell Ackoff and Deming, mid-1980s (A&D)

Video: NBC Whitepaper Special, If Japan Can, Why Can't We? (NBC)

Video: The Deming of America (DoA)

Video: Bill Scherkenbach interviews Deming, 1984 (Video84)

Website: The W. Edwards Deming Institute (WEDI)

All photos in this volume courtesy of The W. Edwards Deming Institute®, deming.org

OTHER BOOKS

... from BetaCodex Press

What would Drucker do?
Niels Pflaeging (editor).
1st ed.

Essays on Beta, Vol. 1
Niels Pflaeging.
1st ed.

Organize for Complexity
Niels Pflaeging.
6th ed.

OpenSpace Beta
Silke Hermann and
Niels Pflaeging. 3rd ed.

Available from your favorite book store –
and also from redforty2.com/shop

Printed in the USA
CPSIA information can be obtained
at www.ICGtesting.com
LVHW071551210823
755851LV00021B/950